LITTLE HISTORIES

Roman Times

Deri Robbins

Kingfisher

Contents

In the beginning…

The first Romans lived in a small, hillside village in the middle of Italy. Over many hundreds of years, the village grew into a great and powerful city with a strong army. In time, this army swept across Europe and North Africa, and into Asia. The lands they ruled over became known as the Roman Empire.

Building an empire

By about 2,000 years ago, the Roman Empire was at its most powerful, and had spread across all of the lands shown in the map below. At this time, the Romans had the best and strongest army in the world.

Whenever they conquered a new country, the Romans built their own forts, roads, bridges and even towns. These were much the same throughout the whole Empire. Apart from the difference in the weather, living in a Roman town in the north of France was just like living in one in Egypt!

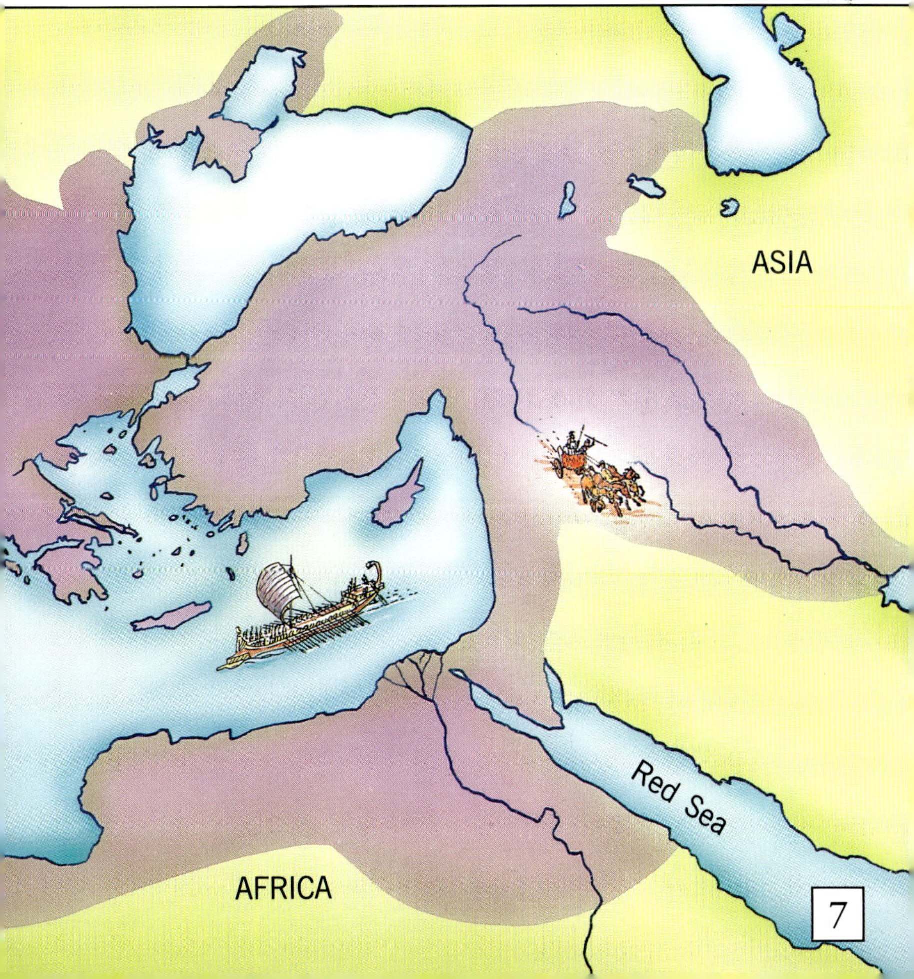

Army life 

Ordinary Roman soldiers were called legionaries. They often had to march long distances, carrying all the armour and the equipment shown below – and still be able to build a camp at the end of the day!

When soldiers needed to stay in one place for a long time, they built a stone fort like this one.

The ruined walls and buildings of some forts can still be seen today, hundreds of years later.

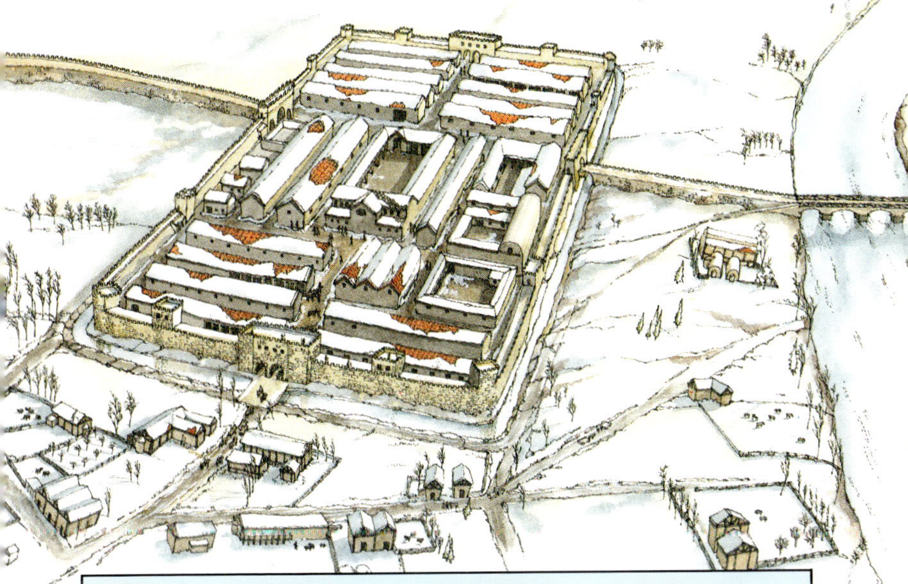

DESIGN A STANDARD

Each troupe of soldiers carried its own standard into battle. Make one from a broom handle, some stiff card, scissors, paper plates, poster paints and glue.

1 Cut a rectangle from the card, then paint it and the paper plates.
2 Glue the plates and the card to the top of the broom handle.

A Roman town

The streets of a Roman town were always laid out in neat, straight lines that formed squares.

KEY

1. Forum
2. Temple
3. Baths
4. Army barracks
5. Theatre
6. Circus
7. Amphitheatre
8. Cemetery
9. Aqueduct
10. Gatehouse
11. Villa

All of the important public buildings were grouped together in the forum, or city centre. Special channels called aqueducts supplied water. The town was surrounded by a high wall with huge gates. Soldiers patrolled the wall day and night.

The town centre

The busiest part of any Roman town was the forum. Market traders would set up their stalls here, and local people would come to find out the latest news and gossip.

Government buildings lined the forum – the most important of these was the basilica, or town hall.

In the middle of the forum was a raised platform, where officials stood to make announcements.

KEY TO THE FORUM

1. Market traders' stalls
2. Treasury
3. The basilica, used as a lawcourt and for other meetings

Street life

The main streets of most Roman towns were crowded, smelly and noisy! Many people lived in blocks of flats, with shops, workshops and taverns on the ground floor. The flats often didn't have kitchens or water.

Many people ate take-away lunches and collected water from a fountain.

Day and night, carts rumbled over the cobbled streets. Some brought supplies to the shops, while others carried building materials – there was always a road somewhere being dug up, or a roof needing repairs!

A house in town

Life was much more comfortable for wealthy Roman families. They lived in large, splendid houses, decorated with mosaics and wall-paintings.

There were usually no windows at all at street level. Instead, all the rooms led into a central open-air hall called the atrium, or a walled garden called the peristyle. Within these two areas the children played and the family met with their guests. Many houses had central heating and some, their own water supply.

① Atrium
② Impluvium (pool)
③ Reception room
④ Kitchen
⑤ Peristyle
⑥ Triclinium (dining room)

MAKE A MOSAIC

1 Sketch a design on to paper or card.
2 Tear up lots of tiny squares from coloured paper.
3 Glue the squares on to the design, leaving little gaps.

Clothing

The Romans dressed simply, in loose, comfortable clothes. Men and children wore tunics, and in the chillier countries of the Empire men often wore tight trousers underneath. Women wore a long dress called a stola, over which they draped a large shawl called a palla.

Men wrapped a cloak called a toga around them, and held it in place at the neck with a brooch. The toga was only worn by freemen, not slaves.

A woman's stola was gathered at the waist and sometimes below the bust as well.

Both men and women wore leather sandals.

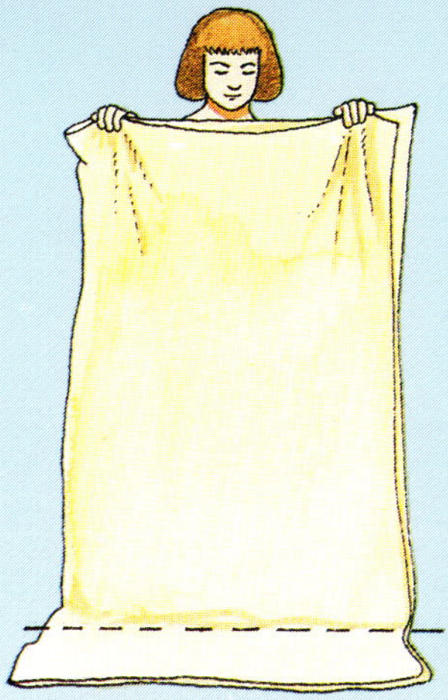

DRESS LIKE A ROMAN

To make a stola, you'll need an old single sheet, some scissors, a needle and thread, six badges or brooches, and string.

1 Fold the sheet in half lengthways and hold it up to your shoulders.

2 Ask someone to trim the sheet about 10 cm below the point where it touches the floor.
3 Sew up the open side of the sheet, and fasten it at the shoulders with the brooches.
4 Slip the stola over your head and tie around the waist.

Make a boy's tunic from a large T-shirt, tied around with string.

You'll need another old single sheet to make a toga. Cut a half-circle out of the sheet – a bit like a cloak – then just drape it over your shoulders.

Eating and drinking

Poor people ate simple food, such as bread and porridge. But richer families often gave lengthy dinner parties where the guests drank wine mixed with water, and feasted on delicacies such as stuffed dormice, roast ostrich and snails soaked in milk! Dinner was served in the triclinium and started at 4 pm.

A ROMAN RECIPE

You'll need: 4 thick slices of bread cut into quarters, milk, 2 tbsp oil, honey.

1 Dip the bread in the milk.

2 Ask an adult to fry the bread in hot oil until crisp, then drain on kitchen paper.

3 Pour honey over the top, and serve.

In the triclinium, people lay on couches around a central table. They ate with their fingers, while the servants brought food in from the kitchen.

Fun and games

After a morning's work, nearly everyone headed for the public baths. These had hot and cold pools, steam rooms, gymnasiums – sometimes there were even libraries!

On public holidays, townspeople flocked to the circus – the huge oval track where horse-drawn chariot races took place. Also popular were the gladiator fights, where men armed with spears and nets, or swords and shields, fought each other – often to the death.

Many charioteers were killed in the races. Those who survived several races were treated like superstars.

The baths were a great meeting place, where people came to relax, exercise and gossip.

The Romans didn't use soap. Instead, people covered themselves with oil and scraped the oil and dirt off with a special tool.

Going to school

Not all children went to school, but the ones who did started when they were about seven years old. The lessons began at dawn and finished early in the afternoon. For writing and maths, children scratched words or sums into wax tablets, using a sharp stick. They learnt to read from scrolls of papyrus, a paper made from reeds.

MAKE A WRITING TABLET

Here's how to make a writing tablet like the ones used by Roman children. You'll need some stiff card, scissors, a craft knife, modelling clay, a rolling pin, a needle and some strong thread.

1 Cut out three pieces of card, the same size. Ask a grown-up to cut the middle out of one to make a frame.

2 Roll out the clay to about 6 mm thick. It should be slightly bigger than the hole in the frame.

3 Put the clay on one piece of card, then glue the frame over the top.

4 Use the needle and thread to attach the final piece of card, like a book cover. Use a sharp pencil to write on your tablet.

A country farm

During the summer, rich families escaped to their grand villas in the countryside. These were often part of a farming estate, and included workshops and houses for the farm workers.

The workers grew grapes, olives and vegetables, as well as caring for the sheep and cattle, and making cheese, wine and olive oil.

Gods and temples

The Romans worshipped a lot of different gods and goddesses, and built separate temples for each of them. The most important gods had temples in the forum.

▷ Every Roman home had a small altar or shrine. The family worshipped there each morning, and left an offering of food and wine on special days.

GODS AND GODDESSES

Here are a few of the most important gods and goddesses worshipped by the Romans.

Jupiter, king of the gods, and his wife, **Juno**.

Minerva, goddess of war.

Mars, god of war.

Venus, goddess of love.

Mercury, messenger of the gods.

Vesta, goddess of the home.

Glossary

amphitheatre – a large, circular building where gladiator fights and other entertainments were put on
aqueduct – a bridge-like channel that carried water
atrium – the hall of a house
baths – where the Romans went to wash, exercise, meet with friends and relax
circus – a large, oval building where chariot races took place
empire – a large area of land ruled by an emperor
forum – a market place or open space, where people held meetings
freeman – someone who is a citizen of a state and not a slave
gladiator – a man trained to fight with other gladiators or with wild animals
legionary – a Roman soldier
mosaic – a pattern made with tiny tiles or stones
peristyle – a walled garden
slave – a person who belongs to someone else, who must do everything their owner says

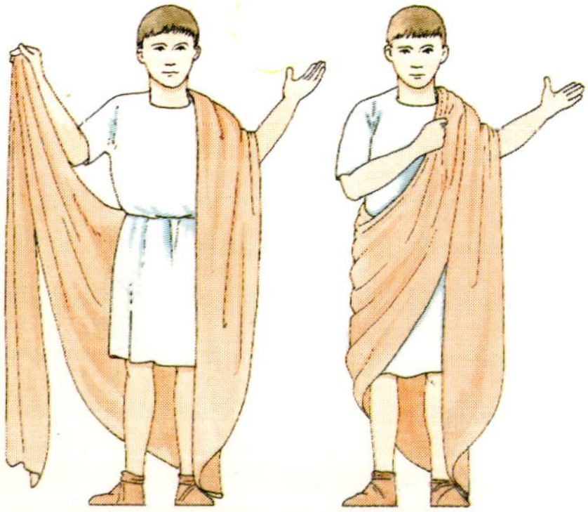